Hear
Me
Out

1

David Nunan
Noriko Tomioka

CENGAGE
Learning®

JN125067

Hear Me Out 1 [Text Only]

Originally written by David Nunan and adapted by Noriko Tomioka

© 2017 Cengage Learning K.K.

Adapted from *Listen In, Book 1, Second Edition* published by National Geographic Learning, a part of Cengage Learning © 2003 Cengage Learning®

Photo Credits:

p. 10: © Jacob Ammentorp Lund/iStock/Thinkstock; p. 18: (l to r) © James Peragine/Hemera/Thinkstock, © Ridofranz/iStock/Thinkstock, © Paffy69/iStock/Thinkstock, © lukas_zb/iStock/Thinkstock, © Wavebreakmedia/iStock/Thinkstock, © shipfactory/iStock/Thinkstock; p. 21: (l to r, t to b) © sodapix sodapix/Thinkstock, © BCFC/iStock/Thinkstock, © cookelma/iStock/Thinkstock, © Digital Vision/DigitalVision/Thinkstock, © SanneBerg/iStock/Thinkstock, © rvbox/iStock/Thinkstock; p. 24: (l to r) © PeopleImages.com/Getty Images, © Mike Watson Images/moodboard/Thinkstock, © Ablestock.com/AbleStock.com/Thinkstock, © Dennis Hallinan/Getty Images; p. 31: (l to r) © Elenathewise/iStock/Thinkstock, © mfron/iStock/Thinkstock, © phogg25/iStock/Thinkstock; p. 33: (l to r) © Zsolt Nyulaszi/Hemera/Thinkstock, © Minerva Studio/iStock/Thinkstock, © monkeybusinessimages/iStock/Thinkstock, © Jupiterimages, Creatas Images/Creatas/Thinkstock; p. 40: (l to r, t to b) © Wavebreakmedia Ltd/Wavebreak Media/Thinkstock, © A_Filiciak/iStock/Thinkstock, © weitao sun/iStock/Thinkstock, © zhudifeng/iStock/Thinkstock, © travelstock44/LOOK-foto/Getty Images, © BananaStock/BananaStock/Thinkstock; p. 43: (l to r, t to b) © Lonely Planet/Getty Images, © Lonely Planet/Getty Images, © thomas hui/iStock/Thinkstock, © Photick/James Hardy/Photick/Thinkstock, © Wilfried Krecichwost/Getty Images, © fazon1/iStock/Thinkstock; p. 52: (l to r) © Ryan McVay/Photodisc/Thinkstock, © Evan Sharboneau/Hemera/Thinkstock, © Ryan McVay/Phontodisc/Thinkstock, © Ohotnik/iStock/Thinkstock; p. 56: (l to r) © Stockbyte/Stockbyte/Thinkstock, © George Doyle/Stockbyte/Thinkstock, © Peter Gudella/iStock/Thinkstock; p. 60: © Wavebreakmedia Ltd/Wavebreak Media/Thinkstock; p. 61: (t to b) © g-stockstudio/iStock/Thinkstock, © Christopher Robbins/Phontodisc/Thinkstock; p. 63: © Huntstock/Thinkstock, © shironosov/iStock/Thinkstock, © Getty Images/Phontodisc/Thinkstock, © Christopher Robbins/Phontodisc/Thinkstock; p. 64: (all) © 2013 National Geographic Learning, a part of Cengage Learning; p. 66: © Steve Mason/Valueline/Thinkstock; p. 69: (l to r) © MaximFesenko/iStock/Thinkstock, © Mypurgatoryyears/iStock/Thinkstock, © Benis Arapovic/Hemera/Thinkstock, © Mike Watson Images/moodboard/Thinkstock; p. 72: (l to r) © Pixland/Pixland/Thinkstock, © warrengoldswain/iStock/Thinkstock, © Mike Watson Images/moodboard/Thinkstock; p. 83: (l to r, t to b) © Nick White/DigitalVision/Thinkstock, © m-imagephotography/iStock/Thinkstock, © Massimo Calmonte (www.massimocalmonte.it)/Getty Images, © DTP/DigitalVision/Thinkstock, © SanneBerg/iStock/Thinkstock, © shironosov/iStock/Thinkstock; p. 84: (l to r) © lukas_zb/iStock/Thinkstock, © amazingmikael/iStock/Thinkstock, © amazingmikael/iStock/Thinkstock, © Jacob Wackerhausen/iStock/Thinkstock; p. 87: (l to r) © Wavebreakmedia Ltd/Wavebreak Media/Thinkstock, © Simon Willms/Phontodisc/Thinkstock, © nikolasvn/iStock/Thinkstock, © Mary Hathaway/iStock/Thinkstock, © Vladimir Arndt/iStock/Thinkstock; p. 93: (l to r, t to b) © Fly_dragonfly/iStock/Thinkstock, © Alexander Raths/iStock/Thinkstock, © Jupiterimages/Goodshoot/Thinkstock, © Christopher Robbins/Phontodisc/Thinkstock, © Jupiterimages/Goodshoot/Thinkstock, © OcusFocus/iStock/Thinkstock, © Mike Watson Images/moodboard/Thinkstock, © monkeybusinessimages/iStock/Thinkstock, © DAJ/Thinkstock; p. 97: (t to b) © VladimirFLoyd/iStock/Thinkstock, © LuminaStock/iStock/Thinkstock, © Monkey Business Images Ltd/Monkey Business/Thinkstock

For permission to use material from this textbook or product, e-mail to **eltjapan@cengage.com**

ISBN: 978-4-86312-317-5

Cengage Learning K.K.
No. 2 Funato Building 5th Floor
1-11-11 Kudankita, Chiyoda-ku
Tokyo 102-0073
Japan

Tel: 03-3511-4392
Fax: 03-3511-4391

はしがき

　以前、初級レベルの学生向けにセンゲージ ラーニングの『Listen In, Book 1』(David Nunan 著) を使用していました。内容が魅力的だったので、いつか機会があれば日本の学生向けにアレンジしたいと思っていたテキストでした。そしてこの度、リスニングシリーズ『Hear Me Out』のレベル 1 (初級) として和書化の依頼をいただき、『Listen In, Book 1』の改編をようやく手がけることになりました。

　本書『Hear Me Out 1』は、その原著となる『Listen In, Book 1』の豊富な音声を最大限に活かし、問題内容も大幅に密度のあるものにしました。この音声にこだわるのは、自然な英語の速さを体感できるからです。この原著の持ち味を活かしつつ、日本の学生がスピード感のある英語でリスニング学習を重ねることにより、自然な英語に馴染めるよう配慮しました。また、同じシリーズの『Hear Me Out 2』に学習がつながるように、平易な問題から難易度を上げた問題に発展させ、学習が進むにつれて次第に聴解力がつくような問題構成となっています。こうした改編の結果、リスニングのテキストとして充実したボリュームのある内容にしたいという思いを本書で実現できました。CD 2 枚分の音声を提供することで、学生による予習そして復習においても聞き応えのある教材となっています。

　各ユニットの導入部は、そのユニットで使われる語彙についての予備演習としています。段階的に平易な問題から難易度を高めながら、多角的に問題を作ったことで、内容理解がよくできるような展開となっています。問題内容に少しくどさを感じるところがあるかもしれません。しかし、何度も音声を耳に馴染ませることにより、最後には音声にしたがってシャドーイングすることができるようになっていただきたいので、聴解力を高めるための繰り返しのトレーニングと理解して学習に臨んでください。

　また、原著に比べると、イラストや写真などが減ったため、ビジュアル的にはシンプルな紙面の仕上がりとなりました。豊富な音声量とそれに付随する問題量によって、集中してリスニングに取り組める工夫がなされています。

　TOEIC や TOEFL などの資格試験に重点が置かれる現在、学生の皆さんがこれらの試験のリスニング問題対策にいきなり取り組むのは難しいでしょう。リスニングが苦手な場合、まずは本書で聴解力を鍛えてから、資格試験のリスニング問題対策に取り組むと良い効果が得られます。この『Hear Me Out 1』が皆さんの英語の聴解力を伸ばす助けになるものと信じます。

　最後に、内容の構成やレイアウトなどにおいて、いろいろな助言をいただき、サポートしてくださったセンゲージ ラーニング株式会社と有限会社パラスタイルの編集担当の方々に心からの謝意を表します。

編著者

音声ファイルの利用方法

ヘッドホン・アイコンがある箇所の音声は、すべてオンラインで再生またはダウンロードすることができます。

https://ngljapan.com/hmo1-audio/

❶上記のURLにアクセス、またはQRコードをスマートフォンなどのリーダーでスキャン

❷表示されるファイル名をクリックして音声ファイルを再生またはダウンロード

Contents

本書の特徴と効果的な使い方

本書は英語の聴解力向上を目指す教材です。テーマ別に分かれた15ユニットから成り、日常的なトピックに沿ったリスニングが中心となっています。1つのユニットは6ページ構成です。各ユニットには6～8つの演習問題（Task）があり、最後のYour Turn! では、そのユニットの学習テーマに沿った内容の会話練習へと発展できるようになっています。

以下では、ユニット内の演習問題やアクティビティの特徴を具体的に述べるとともに、本書の効果的な使用方法を説明します。

---

①

ユニットに出てくる語彙に関する問題です。わからない語彙は辞書で意味を調べ、その語彙が使われている文脈に注意しながら解答を探りましょう。

②～⑧

音声を繰り返し聴き、問題の解答を探っていきます。簡単な導入問題である A から、選択肢問題、内容真偽問題、記述式問題の B や C へと発展していきます。問題をヒントに音声を何回も聴くことで、聴き取った内容の理解を深めていきましょう。じっくりと取り組み、確信が持てる解答が得られるまで、何回も繰り返し聴いてください。

演習問題に取り組むポイント

❶ わからない単語は労力を惜しまず、辞書で意味を調べることが大切です。面倒かもしれませんが、この作業は少しでも意味が頭に残る助けとなります。

❷ これは使える表現だと思ったら、何度も声に出して言ってみたり、何度も書いたりして、自分のものにしていきましょう。このように繰り返し練習することで、英語の表現が豊かになっていきます。

❸ 質問に答える記述式の問題では、英文で解答することに徹します。ただし、文で解答することが難しい場合は、語句で解答しても構いませんが、単語1つだけで解答しないように心がけましょう。

---

① Complete the sentences using the words in the list. Be sure to use the correct form of the word.

| conference | branch | transfer | amazing | convenient | scenery |

1. It is _____ that you won the prize.
2. We closed down our _____ office in Tokyo.
3. It is _____ to have the station so close.
4. We met at an international _____.
5. We admired the beautiful _____ from the hotel balcony.
6. He was _____ from the accounting to the personnel section.

---

③

A Where does each person work now? Listen to the three conversations and match the names to the cities.

Alan — Jakarta
John — Taipei
Chanaboon — Singapore
Kelvin — Bangkok
Greta — San Francisco
Mark — Hong Kong
Pam — New York

B Listen again and circle *T* for *True* or *F* for *False*.

1. John got promoted. T / F
2. John was transferred to Jakarta before he came back to Hong Kong. T / F
3. Greta and Chanaboon met the day before yesterday. T / F
4. Chanaboon has to be in Bangkok by three o'clock. T / F
5. They set up a new office in Singapore. T / F
6. Pam is working in Singapore now. T / F

C Listen again and answer the following questions.

1. Where did Alan and John meet? _____
2. How long was John in Jakarta? _____
3. Where is Chanaboon working? _____
4. Where did Kelvin take over the job for Greta? _____
5. When will Greta visit Bangkok? _____
6. What does Mark think of Shanghai? _____

Your Turn!

Describing what places are like

Sample Dialog

A: Which city do you most want to visit?
B: I really want to see Paris.
A: Oh yeah? Why do you want to go there?
B: Well, it seems like a really exciting place.
A: What would you like to do there?
B: I'd love to visit the Eiffel Tower and go to the Louvre. I've heard Paris is pretty expensive, though.
A: Yeah, but I'm sure you'd enjoy it.

Useful Expressions

- What's **Tokyo** like?
- It's very **big** and **modern**.
- Have you ever been to **Hong Kong**?
- Yes. It's an **interesting** city but very **crowded**.
- Is **Los Angeles** a safe place to live?
- What is there to see and do there?

Try this . . .

Think of three cities you would like to visit. Tell your partner. Ask questions about the cities your partner chose.

My partner's top 3 cities

1. _____
   Why? _____

2. _____
   Why? _____

3. _____
   Why? _____

Your Turn!

いよいよ皆さんが主役になる番です。スピーキングに馴れていなくても、安心してください。会話のサンプルや便利な表現を例示しているので、最初はそれらを使ったり、同じユニット内の演習問題で聴いた会話を参考にしたりして、会話練習をやってみましょう。

●日本語に取り巻かれた環境のなか、英語のリスニング能力を高めることは容易ではありません。初めはまったく聴き取れず、落胆することもあるかと思いますが、聴解力の向上は英語の音声に接する時間数に比例します。さらに効果的に学習を行うには、ただ聞き流すのではなく、演習問題を解きながら、根気よく耳に馴染ませる努力が必要です。音声をよく聴き、あとについてリピートできるくらいまで練習を重ねてください。たとえば、音声ファイルをダウンロードして通学時間を利用して聴いたり、部屋で音楽を聞いて過ごす時間を本書の音声を聴く時間に変えたりするのもよいでしょう。とにかく英語を耳に馴らすことが大切です。初めはなかなか聴き取れませんが、根気よく続けていくと、このテキストでの学習を終える頃には、自分の聴解力の変化にきっと気付くはずです。

1 Complete the sentences using the words in the list. Be sure to use the correct form of the word.

nervous	crowded	heavyset	beard	host	neighbor

1. _____ means having a broad, big, or heavy body.

2. The auditorium was _____ to capacity.

3. Leanne _____ last year's party.

4. I was really _____ before the interview.

5. She had problems with one of her _____ .

6. His features were disguised by dark glasses and a false _____ .

2 Listen and circle the correct response.

1. **a.** No, we're not brothers.
   b. No, just sisters.
   c. No, he's my uncle.

2. **a.** Yes, it is.
   b. I have a wife.
   c. Yes, I do.

3. **a.** Do you have a daughter?
   b. My son is ten.
   c. How old is she?

4. **a.** Two.
   b. I'm the oldest.
   c. Yes, I do.

5. **a.** My brother.
   b. My aunt and uncle.
   c. They sure are.

6. **a.** Do you really?
   b. Are you really?
   c. Can you really?

3 Look at the family tree and complete the sentences below.

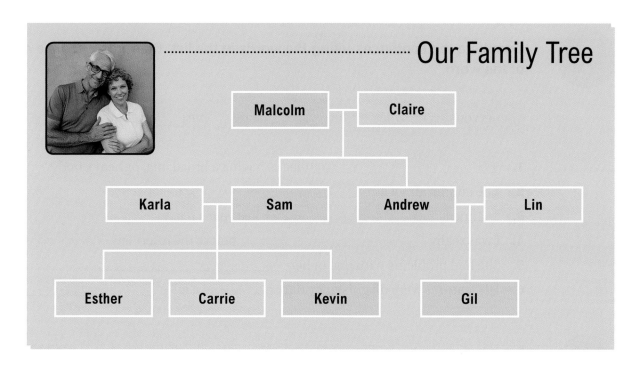

Our Family Tree

Malcolm — Claire

Karla — Sam   Andrew — Lin

Esther   Carrie   Kevin   Gil

1. Malcolm is Claire's _____, Sam's father, and Esther's _____.
2. Esther is Karla's _____ and Carrie's sister.
3. Claire is Sam's _____ and Kevin's _____.
4. Sam is Andrew's _____ and Gil's _____.
5. Kevin is Sam's _____ and Andrew's _____.
6. Karla is Sam's wife and Gil's _____.
7. Kevin is Malcolm's _____ and Gil's _____.
8. Esther is Claire's _____ and Andrew's _____.

4 **A** Listen and circle *T* for *True* or *F* for *False*.

1. Allie has a younger sister.   **T / F**
2. Maggie is Allie's niece.   **T / F**
3. Michelle is Allie's mother.   **T / F**
4. Danny is Allie's son.   **T / F**

B Listen again and complete Allie's family tree.

Doug   Maggie   Bob   Michelle   Danny   Kate

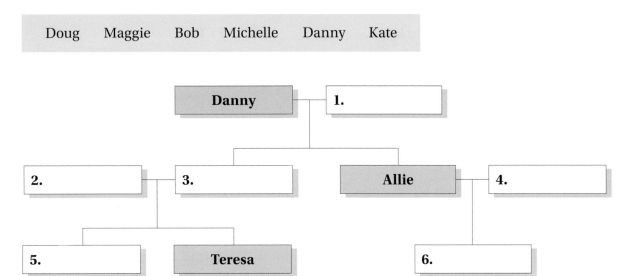

C Listen again and circle the best answer.

1. **a.** Maggie planted a tree for her family.

   b. Maggie planted a tree for her class.

   c. Maggie made the family tree for a class at school.

2. **a.** Allie has a younger brother.

   b. Allie has an older brother.

   c. Allie has an older sister.

3. **a.** Allie's father really wanted a granddaughter.

   b. Allie's father really wanted a grandson.

   c. Allie's father was really happy when Teresa was born.

4. **a.** Allie and Bob are satisfied with just one child.

   b. Allie and Bob aren't satisfied with just one child.

   c. Allie and Bob are expecting a baby.

5

A Listen to Naomi and circle *T* for *True* or *F* for *False*.

1. Naomi is from Japan.   **T / F**
2. She is talking about her own family.   **T / F**
3. One daughter's name is Setsuko.   **T / F**
4. The son's name is Kazuo.   **T / F**
5. Naomi is going to Tokyo.   **T / F**

B Listen again and complete the family tree.

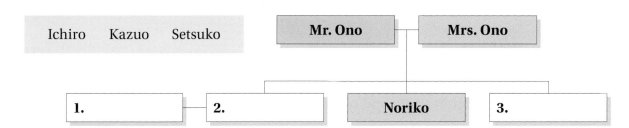

C Listen again and answer the following questions.

1. How long is Naomi going to stay in Japan?   _____
2. When are Setsuko and Kazuo moving into their own house? _____
3. When is Naomi leaving for Osaka?   _____

6

A Anne is talking about some people at a party. Listen and match the names to the relationship words.

[Name]	[Relationship]	[Description]
Harry	cousin	heavyset
Judy	aunt	wearing glasses
Kevin	grandmother	tall
Anne	brother	red shirt
Lyle	father	beard

B Listen again and circle *T* for *True* or *F* for *False*.

1. Since it is a small party, only a few people were invited. **T / F**
2. Anne is helping Walter learn about the people at the party. **T / F**
3. Aunt Judy is next to Harry. **T / F**
4. Aunt Judy is standing behind Lyle. **T / F**

7

A Listen to the conversation between Leanne and John. Write the names of the people they decide to invite to their party.

Guest List	John and Tina Lowe

B Listen again and answer the following questions.

1. What is Leanne planning? _____
2. Why does Leanne ask John to help her make the guest list?

_____

3. Whom does Mike want to meet? _____

8

A Listen and circle the best answer.

1. This is . . .
   a. a face-to-face conversation.
   b. an answering machine message.
   c. a telephone conversation.

2. John's wife . . .
   a. is standing close to the sofa.
   b. is wearing the red dress.
   c. couldn't come to the party.

3. Cathy is . . .
   a. a photographer.
   b. a tennis player.
   c. Mike's friend.

B   **Listen again and fill in the following blanks.**

1. Yumiko is talking with _____.
2. John will introduce Yumiko to his _____ and a few other people.
3. Mike wants to play _____ with Cathy someday.
4. Mike and Alan met at _____ last year.

Your Turn!

Making introductions

Sample Dialog

A: Hi, my name's Tony Kim.
B: Pleased to meet you, Tony. I'm Yumiko Sato.
A: Sorry, your name is Yumiko? How do you spell that?
B: It's Y-U-M-I-K-O. And my last name is Sato. S-A-T-O.
A: Nice to meet you, Yumiko. Are you a friend of John's?
B: No, I'm a friend of Leanne's.

Useful Expressions

- How do you do, **Wendy**?
- Excuse me, are you **Paul King**?
- No, I'm **John Lowe**.
- Do you know **Cathy Chan**?
- Are you a **student**?
- Are you from **Japan**?

Try this . . .

Introduce yourself to three classmates. Find out at least two pieces of information about each one.

	Name	**Information**
Classmate #1		
Classmate #2		
Classmate #3		

Describing someone's appearance and personal traits

1 Complete the sentences using the words in the list.

| prefer | mustache | personnel manager | accountant | flexible | stubborn |

1. He tried various jobs and in the end became an _____.
2. Address your résumé to the _____.
3. Be more _____ in your thinking.
4. I _____ to stay here rather than go alone.
5. He is too _____ to change his mind.
6. His upper lip was covered with a _____.

2 **A** Listen. You will hear a conversation about the five people listed below. Look at the picture and match the names to the correct people (a–e).

- **Cindy Carlyle** _____
- **Charles Markham** _____
- **Elaine Nolan** _____
- **Tony Tan** _____
- **Alan Watts** _____

B Charlotte is identifying some people at an office. Match the names to the positions.

Cindy Carlyle • • accountant

Charles Markham • • personnel manager

Elaine Nolan • • PR guy

Alan Watts • • managing director

C Listen again and circle the best answer.

1. Mr. Markham prefers to be called by . . .
   a. his surname.
   b. his first name.
   c. his nickname.

2. They are going to have . . . from now.
   a. a meeting
   b. an interview
   c. a presentation

3 Listen and circle the correct response.

1. a. No, he's not my father.
   b. No, he's my uncle.
   c. No, my brother is tall.

2. a. Yes, I wear glasses.
   b. Do you wear glasses?
   c. Yes, I see her.

3. a. She's the one in the green shirt.
   b. He's over there.
   c. It's my sister.

4. a. Yes, she is.
   b. I don't know.
   c. She's wearing a jacket.

5. a. Oh, I see him.
   b. Is that her over there?
   c. Does he have a mustache?

6. a. Does he have red hair?
   b. No, he isn't.
   c. Yes, it is.

4

A **Listen and circle the best answer.**

CD1
10

1. The movie director is talking with . . .

   a. an actor.

   b. an agent.

   c. a director.

2. The director wants . . .

   a. three big movie stars.

   b. three million dollars.

   c. three regular actors.

3. He is looking for . . .

   a. three men.

   b. two men and a woman.

   c. two women and a man.

B **What do the actors have to look like? Listen again and circle the correct description for each.**

CD1
10

	M/W	Age	Height	Build	Hair Color
Actor #1	Man Woman	Young Middle-aged Old	Tall Average height Short	Heavyset Average Thin	Brown Blond(e) Red
Actor #2	Man Woman	Young Middle-aged Old	Tall Average height Short	Heavyset Average Thin	Brown Blond(e) Red
Actor #3	Man Woman	Young Middle-aged Old	Tall Average height Short	Heavyset Average Thin	Brown Blond(e) Red

5

A **Match each word to the one with the opposite meaning.**

patient ● ● shy

serious ● ● creative

outgoing ● ● impatient

flexible ● ● talkative

unimaginative ● ● disorganized

quiet ● ● fun-loving

organized ● ● hardworking

lazy ● ● stubborn

B Listen and match the people to the words that describe them. Two words are extra.

Jeffrey

Rae

Gloria

Keith

Irene

Phil

| stubborn | quiet | disorganized | talkative |
| organized | fun-loving | hardworking | lazy |

6 Listen and circle the correct response.

1. a. He started last week.
    b. He's new.
    c. He seems OK.

2. a. She's over there.
    b. Really annoying.
    c. She likes rap music.

3. a. What, the noisy one? Yeah, that's him.
    b. Uh-huh. She's just over there.
    c. He's OK, but he's really noisy.

4. a. Have you met them?
    b. Don't worry, they're really friendly.
    c. Yeah? They're really nice, aren't they?

5. a. Yes, she's really outgoing.
    b. Only when we're with other people.
    c. We're about the same age.

6. a. I'd say I was a bit lazy.
    b. Is she outgoing?
    c. Someone who's hardworking and smart.

7

A Cindy is answering a magazine survey with her boyfriend Kevin. Read the survey. Then listen and circle Kevin's answers.

CD1
18

Personality Survey

1. Do you think of yourself as:
   a. lazy?
   b. hardworking?

2. Are you more frequently:
   a. impatient?
   b. patient?

3. Would you say you are:
   a. fun-loving?
   b. serious?

4. With people, do you tend to be:
   a. stubborn?
   b. flexible?

5. Do you tend to be:
   a. talkative?
   b. quiet?

6. In most situations, are you:
   a. shy?
   b. outgoing?

7. Would you describe yourself as:
   a. organized?
   b. disorganized?

8. Do you consider yourself:
   a. creative?
   b. unimaginative?

B Listen again. Does Cindy agree with Kevin's answers? Circle *A* for *Agree* or *D* for *Disagree*.

CD1
18

1. A / D
2. A / D
3. A / D
4. A / D

5. A / D
6. A / D
7. A / D
8. A / D

Asking and talking about personality traits

Sample Dialog

A: Do you think you're hardworking or lazy?

B: I guess I'm lazy. I really don't like to work hard.

A: So, would you say you're a fun-loving person?

B: Yes. I'm definitely not a very serious person.

A: Why do you think so?

B: Well, I love to go to parties and have a good time.

A: OK. Do you tend to be a stubborn person . . . ?

Useful Expressions

- How would you describe yourself?
- I'm a **hardworking** person but **fun-loving**, too.
- I'm pretty **shy**. I don't really like to **meet new people**.
- What's your new **boyfriend** like?
- Would you say you're a **talkative** person?

Try this . . .

Work with a partner. Role-play the conversation in Task 7 and complete the survey with your partner's information. Give reasons for your answers. Switch roles.

Personality Survey

1. **a.** lazy
   b. hardworking

2. **a.** impatient
   b. patient

3. **a.** fun-loving
   b. serious

4. **a.** stubborn
   b. flexible

5. **a.** talkative
   b. quiet

6. **a.** shy
   b. outgoing

7. **a.** organized
   b. disorganized

8. **a.** creative
   b. unimaginative

1 Complete the sentences using the words in the list. Be sure to use the correct form of the word.

be crazy about	deserve	honor	perform	prayer	exhibition

1. He was _____ with the degree of MA by the university.
2. At last her _____ were answered and she had a child of her own.
3. I think that I _____ this award because I have worked very hard.
4. She will give an _____ of her pictures.
5. I've _____ him since the first time I saw him.
6. They _____ two songs during the encore last night.

2 **A** Listen to each conversation and circle the CD Mick and Marsha talk about.

1.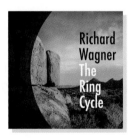

   a.   b.

2.

   a.   b.

3.

   a.   b.

4.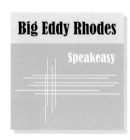

   a.   b.

B Listen again. Does Marsha like or dislike each CD? Circle *Likes* or *Dislikes*.

1. Likes / Dislikes   2. Likes / Dislikes   3. Likes / Dislikes   4. Likes / Dislikes

3 Listen and circle the correct response.

1. **a.** No, she doesn't.
   b. I prefer classical.
   c. Yes, I do.

4. **a.** Classical.
   b. I prefer music.
   c. I like some of his songs.

2. **a.** It's OK.
   b. No, I don't.
   c. I can't stand jazz.

5. **a.** No, I don't.
   b. I don't know. I just don't.
   c. I don't like rock music.

3. **a.** No, it's jazz that I like.
   b. I don't like rock.
   c. I don't mind it.

6. **a.** I love it.
   b. No, I don't.
   c. Me too. She's great.

4

A Listen to the conversation about the Big Audio Awards. Which singers are nominated for Best New Artist? Check (✓) the names.

☐ Kelly King
☐ Jenny Hernandez
☐ Li'l Stevie
☐ Tommy Devlin
☐ Aki Matsumura

B Listen again. Which singers does Randy like? Circle the names above.

5 **A** Listen to the radio broadcast. What does the DJ talk about? Check (✓) the best answer.

CD1 25

☐ The winners of the Big Audio Awards
☐ The nominations for the Big Audio Awards
☐ His choices for the Big Audio Awards

B Listen again. Fill in the blanks with information from the list.

CD1 25

Most Wanted	jazz	Kelly King	rock
Street Fight	pop	*Rough & Smooth*	Sam White

Award Category	Performer	Title	Kind of Music
Best Song	1.	"Love Me Silly"	2.
Best Album	The Glory Hounds	3.	4.
Best Video	5.	6.	rap
Best Soundtrack	7.	*The Other Side of Five*	8.

C Listen again and circle the best answer.

CD1 25

1. Many of the winners won for the (first / second) time, and some were virtually (well-known / unknown).
2. The Glory Hounds also (danced / performed) some of their best known rock hits on the show.
3. Jazz legend Sam White won his (fourth / fifth) Big Audio Award.

A Listen to the announcement and fill in the missing information. For "Place," use the venues in the list below. Two venues are extra.

| City Theater | Wagner Art Gallery | Civic Center |
| Grand Theater | King Club | Metro Gardens |

	Play	**Basketball**	**Concert**	**Party**
Event	The King's Revenge	Knights vs. Towers	City Symphony Orchestra	Video Dance Party
Place	1.	3.	5.	7.
Time	2.	4.	6.	8.

B Listen again and circle the best answer.

1. This is . . .
   a. an official announcement by the government.
   b. an announcement about some of tonight's events.
   c. an announcement about the past events in town.

2. At the City Theater, *Invisible City* will be shown . . .
   a. between 7:00 and 9:30 in the evening.
   b. twice at 7:00 and 9:30 in the morning.
   c. twice at 7:00 and 9:30 in the evening.

3. At the Wagner Art Gallery, an exhibition called *The Gold Rush* opens at . . .
   a. nine.   b. six.   c. ten.

A Listen to the five conversations. Match the conversations (1–5) to the sections of the entertainment guide.

What's On

CONCERTS [ ] **LIVE!**

The Glory Hounds!
Sat/Sun at 8 P.M., South Square Arena

Soul Sisters featuring Rena Robinson
Sat/Sun at 9 P.M., IMG Concert Hall

EXHIBITIONS [ ]

Sandscape: A Display of Egyptian Art
LaSalle Museum. Opens tonight.

Valleyview Sculptors' Society Group Exhibition
Tonight Only! Ford Street Gallery

THEATER [ ]

Siam Sunset
Nightly at 8 P.M., Grove Theater

Social Climbers
Alastair Green's Tony award-winning play
Nightly at 8 P.M., Shakespeare Playhouse

MOVIES [ ]

Quarantine!
Evening shows at 7: 30 & 9: 45, Bijou Theater

The Devil's Playground
Six shows daily, Capitol Theater

Midnight Double Feature!
Sleep of the Dead 2 & Mad Hatter III
Bayside Multiplex

CLUBS [ ]

DJ Jinx Dance Party
Every Sat at 10 P.M., Slider's Music Club

Glam Rock Party
Weekends, Midnight–6 A.M., Club 64

Line Dancing Party
Every Fri/Sat at 9 P.M., Bob's Country Bunker

B Listen again. For each conversation, circle the event the people plan to attend.

C Listen again and answer the following questions about each conversation.

1. On what day are they going to the concert? _____

2. What play did Marcie see? _____

3. How long will the Sandscape exhibition be open? _____

4. What time will Gloria and Bob meet Gina? _____

5. Why couldn't Tim get tickets for the horror double feature at the Bayside?
_____

Your Turn!

Talking about music preferences

Sample Dialog

A: Hey, Jeff, do you like U2?

B: Oh yeah. They're fantastic!

A: What's your favorite song?

B: Let me think . . . I really like "Sunday Bloody Sunday."

A: Oh really? I prefer "I Still Haven't Found What I'm Looking For."

Useful Expressions

- Who's your favorite **singer**?
- What kind of music do you like?
- I really like **jazz**.
- Me too. What do you think of **Miles Davis**?
- How do you feel about **rap**?
- I don't mind it, but I prefer **rock**.

Try this . . .

Make a list of your three favorite musical performers. Ask your partner for his/her opinion and check (✓) *Yes* or *No*. Find out your partner's favorite song by that performer or the name of a performer your partner prefers.

	My Top Performers	Partner likes?
1.		☐ Yes / Favorite song: ☐ No / Prefers:
2.		☐ Yes / Favorite song: ☐ No / Prefers:
3.		☐ Yes / Favorite song: ☐ No / Prefers:

Describing what places are like

1 Complete the sentences using the words in the list. Be sure to use the correct form of the word.

| conference | branch | transfer | amazing | convenient | scenery |

1. It is _____ that you won the prize.
2. We closed down our _____ office in Tokyo.
3. It is _____ to have the station so close.
4. We met at an international _____.
5. We admired the beautiful _____ from the hotel balcony.
6. He was _____ from the accounting to the personnel section.

2 Match each word to the one with the opposite meaning.

small ○   ○ modern
noisy ○   ○ beautiful
traditional ○   ○ relaxing
dangerous ○   ○ big
ugly ○   ○ exciting
stressful ○   ○ safe
boring ○   ○ inexpensive
expensive ○   ○ quiet

3

A **Where does each person work now? Listen to the three conversations and match the names to the cities.**

Alan   Jakarta
John   Taipei
Chanaboon   Singapore
Kelvin   Bangkok
Greta   San Francisco
Mark   Hong Kong
Pam   New York

B **Listen again and circle *T* for *True* or *F* for *False*.**

1. John got promoted.   **T / F**
2. John was transferred to Jakarta before he came back to Hong Kong.   **T / F**
3. Greta and Chanaboon met the day before yesterday.   **T / F**
4. Chanaboon has to be in Bangkok by three o'clock.   **T / F**
5. They set up a new office in Singapore.   **T / F**
6. Pam is working in Singapore now.   **T / F**

C **Listen again and answer the following questions.**

1. Where did Alan and John meet?   _____

2. How long was John in Jakarta?   _____

3. Where is Chanaboon working?   _____

4. Where did Kelvin take over the job for Greta?   _____

5. When will Greta visit Bangkok?   _____

6. What does Mark think of Shanghai?   _____

A How does Dave describe each city? Listen and match each word to the correct city.

CD1
35

interesting •

big •

safe •   • Bangkok

convenient •   • Seoul

exciting •   • Singapore

clean •   • Tokyo

modern •

inexpensive •

B Listen again and fill in the following blanks.

CD1
35

1. The man is being _____ to Asia from the New York office.

2. The man asked Dave to give him some _____.

3. There are some amazing _____ in Bangkok.

4. Singapore is very convenient to get _____.

C Listen again and circle the best answer.

CD1
35

1. They are talking at . . .
   a. a trade exhibition.
   b. a sales conference.
   c. a sales seminar.

2. Dave knows much about Asia since he . . .
   a. has some experience as a tour guide in Asia.
   b. has worked in some offices in Asia.
   c. has worked in all the offices in Asia.

3. Dave was studying . . . when he was in Asia.
   a. Buddhism
   b. Hinduism
   c. Buddhist temples

5   Listen and circle the correct response.

1.   **a.**   Taipei.
    b.   Yeah, that's right.
    c.   I'm from Taipei.

2.   **a.**   New York, actually.
    b.   Yes, she does.
    c.   Yes, I am.

3.   **a.**   Yes, it is.
    b.   Yes, I do.
    c.   Yes, I am.

4.   **a.**   No, I'm not.
    b.   Yes, it is.
    c.   Seoul.

5.   **a.**   Yes, it is.
    b.   Big.
    c.   I like big cities.

6.   **a.**   Yeah, but it's quite expensive.
    b.   Yeah, but it's really exciting.
    c.   Yeah, but I'm sure you'd like it.

6   **A**   Listen and circle *T* for *True* or *F* for *False*.

1.   Min-hee is thinking about taking a vacation in the United States.   **T / F**
2.   Evan has been to all three cities.   **T / F**
3.   Evan's hometown is San Francisco.   **T / F**
4.   Min-hee has been to San Francisco.   **T / F**
5.   Min-hee doesn't know much about the schools.   **T / F**

B   Listen again. Check (✓) the words Evan uses to describe each city.

City	beautiful	clean	exciting	expensive	interesting	modern	quiet
San Francisco							
Salt Lake City							
Boston							

7

A Listen and circle the best answer.

1. Jiro visited Canada . . .
   a. for a business meeting.
   b. to study English.
   c. to visit his family.

2. He went to the top of the . . .
   a. Calgary Tower.
   b. Cabot Tower.
   c. CN Tower.

3. His favorite city is . . .
   a. Toronto.
   b. Vancouver.
   c. Banff.

B Listen again. Check (✓) the words Jiro uses to describe each city.

Vancouver

Toronto

Banff

☐ expensive
☐ boring
☐ exciting
☐ safe

☐ modern
☐ quiet
☐ big
☐ relaxing

☐ traditional
☐ beautiful
☐ stressful
☐ small

C Listen again and answer the following questions.

1. How long was Jiro in Canada? _____

2. What did Jiro do in Toronto? _____

3. What has Emily heard about Banff? _____

Your Turn!

Describing what places are like

Sample Dialog

A: Which city do you most want to visit?
B: I really want to see Paris.
A: Oh yeah? Why do you want to go there?
B: Well, it seems like a really exciting place.
A: What would you like to do there?
B: I'd love to visit the Eiffel Tower and go to the Louvre. I've heard Paris is pretty expensive, though.
A: Yeah, but I'm sure you'd enjoy it.

Useful Expressions

- What's **Tokyo** like?
- It's very **big** and **modern**.
- Have you ever been to **Hong Kong**?
- Yes. It's an **interesting** city but very **crowded**.
- Is **Los Angeles** a safe place to live?
- What is there to see and do there?

Try this . . .

Think of three cities you would like to visit. Tell your partner. Ask questions about the cities your partner chose.

My partner's top 3 cities

1. _____

   Why? _____

2. _____

   Why? _____

3. _____

   Why? _____

1

Complete the sentences using the words in the list. Be sure to use the correct form of the word.

| lawyer | criminal | mechanic | take charge of | résumé | correction |

1. The _____ crawled out from under the car.
2. According to his _____, the candidate graduated from university in 2010.
3. You should seek advice from your _____ on this matter.
4. A few small errors need _____.
5. I'll _____ planning for the trip.
6. _____ often return to the scene of the crime.

2

A **Listen to the four conversations and match the conversations (1–4) to the photos (a–d).**

1. ____   2. ____   3. ____   4. ____

 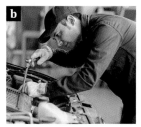  

_____   _____   _____   _____

B **Listen again and use the words in the list to show each occupation. Two words are extra.**

| teacher | police officer | mechanic | social worker |
| journalist | computer programmer | | |

C **Listen again and circle the best answer.**

1. Steve got his first computer when he was about . . .

   a. nine years old.

   b. ten years old.

   c. twelve years old.

2. He thinks computer programming is a creative job because he can . . .

   a. create whatever he wants.

   b. realize whatever he imagines.

   c. make something from nothing.

3. Margo wanted to be . . . when she was a high school student.

   a. a lawyer

   b. a police officer

   c. a bodyguard

4. She feels her present job is . . .

   a. dangerous.

   b. boring.

   c. challenging.

5. The man left the trucking company because he didn't want to . . .

   a. deliver things.

   b. work overtime.

   c. do oil changes.

6. He wants to . . .

   a. work for a trucking company.

   b. do any job when he is asked.

   c. work on engines.

7. Mark wants to go into education because he enjoyed . . .

    a. his part-time job at a cram school.

    b. his part-time job as a tutor.

    c. the teaching practice.

8. He expects . . . from the job.

    a. a lot of income

    b. high social status

    c. job satisfaction

Listen and circle the correct response.

CD1 / 43

1. **a.** I'm a teacher.

   b. Are you a teacher?

   c. Falls City High School.

4. **a.** Carlson Street.

   b. The hours are long.

   c. For about three years.

2. **a.** As a waiter.

   b. Hudson Accounting.

   c. Monday to Friday.

5. **a.** I don't know.

   b. Yes, I speak Spanish.

   c. I can write it.

3. **a.** Yes, I like it.

   b. For two years.

   c. Yes, I can.

6. **a.** 40 words a minute.

   b. Yes, I can type.

   c. $40 an hour.

4   **A**   **Listen and circle the best answer.**

CD1 / 44

1. Lucy asks about a . . .

   a. newspaper interview.

   b. job interview.

   c. college interview.

2. Lucy's appointment is for . . .

   a. 2:00.

   b. 2:30.

   c. 2:45.

3. Lucy talks to . . .

   a. Paula.

   b. Barbara.

   c. Conrad.

B Listen again and check (✓) Lucy's answers.

Name:	Lucy Turner		
Position wanted:	☐ Editor	☐ Designer	☐ Writer
Computer skills:	☐ PictureShop	☐ DesignWiz	☐ Exalt 2.0
Languages:	☐ French	☐ German	☐ Japanese
Availability:	☐ Days	☐ Evenings	☐ Weekends

A Listen to the four conversations and circle the things Alison can do.

1. **a.** type 60 words a minute
    b. type 70 words a minute
    c. type 75 words a minute

2. **a.** use the coffee machine
    b. use the phone system
    c. use the fax machine

3. **a.** speak French
    b. speak Spanish
    c. speak Chinese

4. **a.** use PictureShop software
    b. use AccountBook software
    c. use Exalt software

B Listen again and circle *T* for *True* or *F* for *False*.

1. Mr. Lee wants to find someone who can type, answer the phone, and help out wherever else when it's necessary.   **T / F**
2. Alison has just finished the order form.   **T / F**
3. Mr. Woo needs someone who can speak Chinese.   **T / F**
4. Alison forgot how to use a spreadsheet program.   **T / F**

A Read the job ad. Then listen to the two job interviews. Write *Yes* or *No* for each item on the interview form.

WANTED

Paris-based fashion/lifestyle magazine seeks experienced designer to supervise layout and design team. Computer design skills essential. Must be bilingual.

E-mail résumé to **editor@fashionparis.co.fr**

Job Interview Form

		Patricia	Julian
a.	Can use DesignWiz software		
b.	Can take professional photos		
c.	Can speak and write French		
d.	Can type 60 words per minute		
e.	Can work with spreadsheets		
f.	Can work weekends		
g.	Can travel overseas		

B Listen again and circle the best answer.

1. Patricia began her career as a/an . . . at *Q-style* magazine.
   a. senior designer
   b. photographer
   c. intern

2. Patricia is better at speaking French than . . .
   a. translating.
   b. writing.
   c. reading.

3. Julian has worked for *Fashion Central* magazine for . . .
   a. two years.
   b. three years.
   c. four years.

4. Julian studied . . . before he got into design.
   a. photography
   b. design
   c. accounting

Your Turn!

Asking and answering job interview questions

Sample Dialog

A: We're looking for someone with computer design skills.

B: I can use DesignWiz software. I also know PictureShop.

A: OK. Can you work with spreadsheets?

B: Yes, I used spreadsheets in my previous job.

A: What about your language skills? Can you speak French?

B: Yes, I can. I studied in France for three years. I love to travel.

A: That's great. I just have a few more questions.

Useful Expressions

- Why did you leave your last job?
- I was **looking for a new challenge**.
- Why do you think you're the best candidate for the job?
- I have **a lot of experience** and I'm very **hardworking**.
- Are you willing to **travel** or **move to another city**?
- Yes, **I love to travel** and **I'd be willing to relocate**.

Try this . . .

Work with a partner. Role-play the job interview in Task 6. Take notes on your partner's job qualifications. Switch roles.

Job Interview Form

- **Personal qualities:** _____

_____

- **Job skills:** _____

_____

- **Language skills:** _____

_____

- **Availability:** _____

_____

1 Complete the sentences using the words in the list. Be sure to use the correct form of the word.

| concentration | brochure | fortune-teller | drugstore | brief | fascinating |

1. You can find this medicine in supermarkets and _____.
2. The information is given in the _____.
3. She met a _____ man at the party.
4. We had a _____ conversation as we passed each other.
5. I find it impossible to believe what that _____ says.
6. There are many ways to improve your _____ while studying.

2 Read the statements (1–5). Use the information in the brochure to decide which hotel each statement describes.

1. It's close to a major shopping center. → _____
2. It's across from a ferry terminal. → _____
3. It's near several movie theaters. → _____
4. It's between two subway stations. → _____
5. It's beside a zoo. → _____

Welcome to Hong Kong!

Make the most of your stay by booking into one of these popular downtown hotels.

Mandarin Oriental

Conveniently located opposite the Star Ferry Terminal.

Conrad Hong Kong

Just by the Conrad is Pacific Place, one of Hong Kong's largest shopping complexes.

Park Lane

Located beside Victoria Park, close to the Pearl, Jade, and Windsor Cinemas.

Eaton Hotel Hong Kong

Just a short walk from Jordan MTR station to the south and Yau Ma Tei MTR station to the north.

YMCA Garden View International House

Located next to the Zoological & Botanical Gardens, home to hundreds of different kinds of birds and animals.

3

1. _____   2. _____   3. _____   4. _____   5. _____   6. _____

☐ Pacific Place   ☐ Victoria Harbour   ☐ Hong Kong Arts Centre

☐ Times Square   ☐ Aberdeen Harbour   ☐ Hong Kong Cultural Centre

☐ King's Park   ☐ Tin Hau Temple   ☐ Citibank Plaza

☐ Kowloon Park   ☐ Man Mo Temple   ☐ Bank of America Tower

B Listen again. Where is each person advised to go? Check (✓) the correct place below each photo.

C Listen again and circle the best answer for each conversation.

1. Tai Chi is a martial art which improves your concentration and helps you . . .
   a. relax.
   b. arouse your fighting instinct.
   c. arouse your combative spirit.

2. The woman is looking for a . . . on cultural events in Hong Kong.
   a. book
   b. brochure
   c. guide book

3. They are looking for a place to . . .

   a. hear live music.

   b. see a musical.

   c. dance.

4. The woman's husband wants to . . .

   a. make a fortune.

   b. buy a lottery ticket.

   c. consult a fortune-teller.

5. The woman is looking for somewhere . . .

   a. to change money.

   b. for a change.

   c. to shop.

6. On a huge floating platform on the water, there are . . .

   a. restaurants.

   b. markets.

   c. stages.

4 **Listen to the directions and circle _T_ for _True_ or _F_ for _False_.**

1. The drugstore is across from the church.   **T / F**
2. The hotel is in front of the bookstore.   **T / F**
3. The market is next to the hospital.   **T / F**
4. The subway station is on Kensington Street.   **T / F**
5. The movie theater is across from the mall.   **T / F**

5 **A** **Listen to the telephone recording. Match each place to its location (a–h) on the map. Three locations are extra.**

- **Papa Romano's Restaurant**

  _____

- **Hollywood Theater**

  _____

- **Sunnyvale Shopping Center**

  _____

- **City Center Subway Station**

  _____

- **Bus Station**

  _____

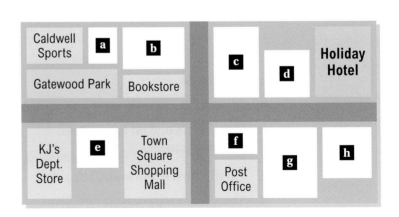

B **Listen again and fill in the following blanks.**

1. Papa Romano's restaurant is _____ the hotel.
2. Hollywood Theater is _____ Gatewood Park.
3. Town Square Shopping Mall is _____ the bookstore.
4. Sunnyvale Shopping Center is _____ the hotel.
5. City Center subway station is located _____ Town Square Shopping Mall and K.J.'s Department Store.
6. Buses are available at the bus station _____ the post office.

C **Listen again and circle *T* for *True* or *F* for *False*.**

1. This is a public announcement.   **T / F**
2. Papa Romano's Restaurant is Italian.   **T / F**
3. Hollywood Theater is a cinema complex.   **T / F**
4. At the bus station you can find a route map.   **T / F**

6   **Listen and circle the correct response.**

1. a. I'm going shopping.
    b. It's next to the ferry terminal.
    c. Yes, there is.

2. a. Yes, we do.
    b. It's near the hotel.
    c. Yes, there's one on Ridge Road.

3. a. Go to Third Avenue and turn right.
    b. Yes, there's a park near here.
    c. The park opens at nine.

4. a. The museum is on the right.
    b. For about two years.
    c. At 10:00.

5. a. No, the hotel is open.
    b. No, it's right across the street.
    c. No, it's a hotel.

6. a. It's close to the hotel.
    b. Italian food.
    c. There are some on Watt Street.

7

A Listen to the tourist information about Kowloon. Put the places (a–f) in the order that you hear them.

CD1 64

1. _c_   2. ____   3. ____   4. ____   5. ____   6. ____

Museum of History   **Knutsford Terrace**
____   ____

Peninsula Hotel   **Bird Market**
_k_   ____

Space Museum   **Night Market**
____   ____

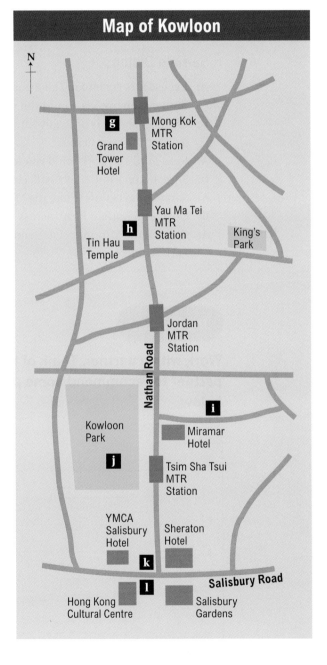

Map of Kowloon

N

Mong Kok MTR Station

g Grand Tower Hotel

Yau Ma Tei MTR Station

h Tin Hau Temple

King's Park

Jordan MTR Station

Nathan Road

i

Kowloon Park

Miramar Hotel

j

Tsim Sha Tsui MTR Station

YMCA Salisbury Hotel

Sheraton Hotel

k

l Salisbury Road

Hong Kong Cultural Centre

Salisbury Gardens

B Listen again. Match each place to its location (g–l) on the map.

CD1 64

Your Turn!

Asking for directions and describing locations

Sample Dialog

A: Excuse me, I'm looking for a good place to have dinner with friends. Could you recommend a place?

B: The best choice is probably Knutsford Terrace. It isn't too far from here.

A: Knutsford Terrace? Could you tell me where that is?

B: Sure. It's on Kimberley Road, close to the Miramar.

A: Sorry. I don't know where the Miramar is.

B: Oh, it's on Nathan Road, across from Kowloon Park.

A: Close to the Miramar Hotel, across from Kowloon Park. Thanks.

Useful Expressions

- Excuse me, is there a **post office** near here?
- Sure. Go up **Nathan Road** to **Middle Road** and turn **right**.
- Is the **Causeway Centre** in **Kowloon**?
- No, it's not. It's in **Wanchai**.
- Is it within walking distance from here?
- No, you should probably **take a cab**.

Try this . . .

Work with a partner. Think of three things you'd like to do in Kowloon. Ask your partner to recommend some places and give you directions. Take notes in the space below.

1 Complete the sentences using the words in the list. Be sure to use the correct form of the word.

| furniture | cashier | restroom | luggage | take advantage of | locate |

1. Airlines limit the amount of _____ that travelers can take on board.
2. The office is _____ on the first floor.
3. I handed the _____ a $10 bill.
4. Students should _____ the university's facilities.
5. There is a lot of _____ in his room.
6. This _____ is for the physically handicapped.

2 **A** **Look at the sale signs. Write the correct floor number for each sale.**

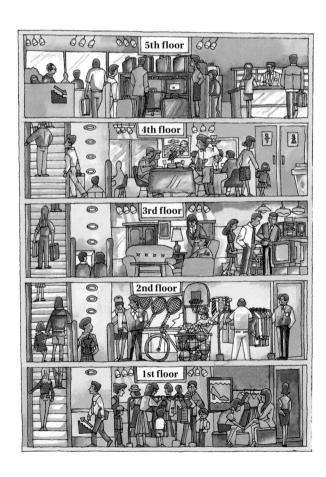

1. Low, Low Prices on Basketballs!
   → _____ floor

2. Great Discounts on Summer Clothes!
   → _____ floor

3. 20% Off on All Woofer Stereos!
   → _____ floor

4. Huge Armchair Clearout!
   → _____ floor

5. One Day Only! Specials on Suitcases!
   → _____ floor

6. 2 for 1 Sale on All Neckties!
   → _____ floor

B **Match the words in the list to the departments (a–j) in a store.**

cashier	children's wear
electrical goods	furniture
luggage	men's wear
restaurant	restrooms
sporting goods	women's shoes

a. _____

b. _____

c. _____

d. _____

e. _____

f. _____

g. _____

h. _____

i. _____

j. _____

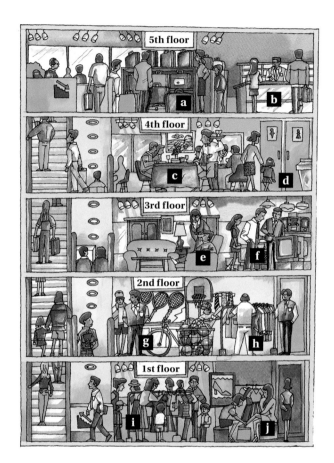

3 **Listen and complete the following sentences with _in_, _on_, _next to_, or _between_.**

1. Men's wear is _____ the second floor.

2. CD players are _____ the electrical goods department.

3. The electrical goods department is _____ the furniture department.

4. Tennis rackets are _____ the second floor in sporting goods.

5. Sporting goods are _____ the restaurant and the escalator.

4

A **Listen to the elevator announcement and circle the best answer.**

1. The sporting goods department is on the . . . floor.

    a. second   **b.** third   **c.** fifth

2. The . . . department is on the seventh floor.

    a. men's wear   **b.** women's wear   **c.** children's wear

3. The electronic goods department is on the . . . floor.

    a. second   **b.** third   **c.** fifth

4. The . . . department is on the fifth floor.

    a. electrical goods   **b.** sporting goods   **c.** furniture

B **Listen again and complete the following scripts.**

1. . . . track suits, _tennis rackets_, soccer balls, roller blades, and

    _____ . . .

2. . . . _____, shorts, _____, _____,

    and hats . . .

3. . . . _____, VCRs, _____, microwaves, and MD

    players . . .

4. . . . sofas, _____, chairs, _____, and

    _____ . . .

5 Listen and circle the number you hear.

1. second / seventh
2. eight / eighth

3. sixth / six
4. first / fourth

5. nine / ninth
6. thirteen / thirteenth

6 Listen and circle the correct response.

1. a. Sporting goods? On the second floor.
   b. It's next to the sporting goods department.
   c. No, I don't see them.

2. a. Yes, this is the women's wear department.
   b. Children's wear is on the fourth floor.
   c. No, it's on the fourth floor.

3. a. Next to the toy department.
   b. The electrical goods department.
   c. Electrical goods are on the fifth floor.

4. a. I'm looking for the restrooms.
   b. Yes, there's a restaurant on the fourth floor.
   c. Yes, they're next to the travel goods department.

5. a. Women's wear and shoes.
   b. Women's wear is on sale.
   c. Women's wear is on the second floor.

6. a. No, there are no toys in sporting goods.
   b. No, but there's a toy store across the street.
   c. No, Dad is in the toy department.

A Listen to the public address announcement and match the departments to their locations (a–g) at Shoprite Discount Warehouse.

CD1 77

- **electrical goods** _____
- **women's wear** _____
- **sporting goods** _____
- **furniture** _____
- **men's wear** _____
- **children's wear** _____
- **luggage** _____

4th floor

3rd floor

2nd floor

1st floor

Legend:
$: ATM
: women's restroom
: men's restroom

B Listen again and check (✓) the departments where there are special offers.

CD1 77

☐ electrical goods   ☐ women's wear   ☐ sporting goods   ☐ furniture
☐ men's wear   ☐ children's wear ☐ luggage

C Listen again and circle *T* for *True* or *F* for *False*.

CD1 77

1. Cosmetics are on the first floor.   **T / F**
2. Hardware is next to men's wear.   **T / F**
3. The sale on women's skirts lasts two weeks.   **T / F**
4. The food court is next to furniture.   **T / F**
5. If you are a Frequent Shoppers Club member,   **T / F**
   you can get some discounts on TVs.

Your Turn!

Talking about locations in a store

Sample Dialog

A: Can I help you?

B: Yes, I'm looking for running shoes.

A: Running shoes? Right over there in the sporting goods department.

B: Great. I'm also looking for a skirt for my wife.

A: OK. Women's wear is on the third floor next to the children's wear department. You can take the escalator.

B: And where's that?

A: Right next to hardware.

Useful Expressions

- Excuse me. Can you tell me where to find **CD players**?
- Sure. They're **right upstairs** in the **electrical goods** department.
- Take the **escalator to four** and it's **right next to the food court**.
- What floor is **sporting goods** on?
- Is there a **restroom** on this floor?

Try this . . .

Write the names of five friends or family members and think of a gift you'd like to buy for each person. Tell a partner what you're looking for. Ask where you can find each item at Shoprite Discount Warehouse.

	Name	Gift
1.		
2.		
3.		
4.		
5.		

1 Complete the sentences using the words in the list. Be sure to use the correct form of the word.

| figure out | throw out | depend on | hook up | cursor | take a look at |

1. Check that the computer is _____ to the printer.
2. Move your _____ to the top of the screen.
3. Why don't you _____ all this garbage?
4. Let's _____ this picture.
5. Japan _____ foreign countries for oil.
6. I couldn't _____ the solution to the math problem.

2 Write the correct instruction in the list under each picture.

_____ _____ _____ _____

_____ _____ _____ _____

| Put in | Open | Press | Adjust | Turn on | Plug in | Click | Move |

3

A Listen and circle the words you hear in each conversation.

1. Press / Put in / Click / Move / Open / Adjust / Close / Plug in
2. Press / Put in / Move / Open / Close / Adjust / Turn on / Take out
3. Press / Put in / Click / Move / Open / Plug in / Turn on / Take out

B Listen again. Which item is being talked about? Match the conversations (1–3) to the items (a–c).

1. _____   2. _____   3. _____

4

A Gerald is calling a Help Line to get instructions for his MD player. Listen and write *Do* or *Don't* for each instruction.

1. _____ plug the cable into the "phones" slot.
2. _____ put a disc in the MD player.
3. _____ close the cover on the MD player.
4. _____ press "Record" on the MD player.
5. _____ adjust the volume.
6. _____ keep recording until the CD stops playing.

B **Listen again and circle the best answer.**

CD1
81

1. What problem does the man have with his F-100 model?

    a. The man can't record some part of a CD.

    b. The man can't make a copy of a CD on the MD player.

    c. The man can't play a whole CD.

2. What does the man have to do after he turns on the CD and MD players?

    a. He has to connect the MD player and the CD player correctly.

    b. He has to leave the recording process to the MD player.

    c. He has to wait until the CD and MD players turn off automatically.

3. What does the man have to do when the MD player begins to record?

    a. After he presses "Record" on the MD player, he doesn't have to do anything.

    b. He has to record at the right level.

    c. He has to adjust the volume of the CD player.

Listen and circle the correct response.

CD1
82

1. a. It's a computer.

    b. First, you plug it in.

    c. Yes, it does.

2. a. It opens the cover.

    b. Press the "Power" button.

    c. You have to turn it on.

3. a. Yes, you do.

    b. Here is the CD.

    c. Put it in here.

4. a. This is the "Off" button.

    b. No, over here.

    c. Yes, it is.

5. a. Just press this button.

    b. Don't turn it on.

    c. Take out the tape.

6. a. That's the next step.

    b. Yes, you do.

    c. Click on an icon.

6

A   **Listen and circle the best answer.**

1. This is a conversation between . . .

    a. two co-workers.

    b. two friends.

    c. two teachers.

2. PictureDisc is . . .

    a. a CD-ROM.

    b. a web site.

    c. a newsletter.

3. Pete describes how to . . .

    a. use a camera to take a photo.

    b. download a photo from the Internet.

    c. design a new web site.

B   **Listen again and number the instructions (1–7).**

_____ Click on the photo.

_____ Type a file name.

_____ Use the search engine to look for photos.

_____ Type your name and employee number.

_____ Press "Save" to store it on your computer.

_____ Open the catalog page.

_____ Choose "Save Picture As . . . "

7

A   **Listen and check (✓) the best statement.**

☐ The man learns how to look at the photos on his digital camera.

☐ The man learns how to download photos from his digital camera.

☐ The man learns how to take photos using his digital camera.

B Listen again and number the pictures (a–f) in the order you hear the instructions.

CD1
84

1. _____   2. _____   3. _____   4. _____   5. _____   6. _____

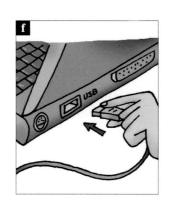

C Listen again and fill in the following blanks.

CD1
84

1. To look at the photos on the computer screen, you have to _____ the cable between the camera and computer.

2. To download photos, _____ the "Mode" dial to "Connect."

3. After the pictures are downloaded, _____ the camera and the photos are on the screen.

Giving and understanding instructions

Sample Dialog

A: Can you tell me how to use this computer?

B: Sure. First you have to turn it on. Just press the "Power" button.

A: OK. Do I have to open this now?

B: Yes. Open it, put in a disk, and then close it.

A: How do I open it? Do I press a button on the right side?

B: No, the button is on the front. You adjust the sound on the side.

Useful Expressions

- How do I **turn it on**?
- I don't know how to **open** it.
- What is this **cable** for?
- **Move this switch** to **adjust the picture quality**.
- You have to **use the slot marked "Cable In."**

Try this . . .

Choose an electronic item from the ones shown. Ask your partner how to use it. Repeat the instructions to your partner and then switch roles.

1 Complete the sentences using the words in the list. Be sure to use the correct form of the word.

routine	workout	semester	unwind	run out of	on one's way

1. Listening to music helps me _____ after a busy day.

2. I added jogging to my daily _____.

3. The machine is _____ fuel, so we need to get some soon.

4. This _____ helps you burn off fat and tone muscles.

5. Will you pick up some food at the supermarket _____ home?

6. I'm taking seven lecture courses this _____.

2

A Listen to the six statements. Match the statements (1–6) to the clocks (a–f).

1. _____
2. _____
3. _____
4. _____
5. _____
6. _____

B Listen again and write the verb you hear under each clock.

The pictures show the activities in Nathan's daily routine. Fill in the blanks with the times to match the pictures.

1. Nathan gets up at _eight forty-five_.

2. He does his homework at _____.

3. He gets to school at _____.

4. He has lunch at _____.

5. He goes to the gym at _____.

6. He eats dinner at _____.

7. He watches TV with his friends at _____.

8. He plays pool with his friends at _____.

9. He goes to bed at _____.

4 Listen to the five questions and circle the best response.

1. a. Oh, about eight thirty.
   b. About noon.

2. a. At five thirty.
   b. Twelve thirty.

3. a. Around six thirty.
   b. Oh, around two.

4. a. Three o'clock.
   b. Seven o'clock.

5. a. Around six thirty.
   b. Usually around eleven.

5 Listen and circle the correct response.

1. a. Yes, I do.
   b. Every day.
   c. Around four-thirty.

2. a. At 9:00.
   b. I get to school about 9:00.
   c. Yes, they usually do.

3. a. I'm busy this Saturday.
   b. I eat lunch.
   c. I clean the house.

4. a. About forty-five minutes.
   b. Twelve-thirty.
   c. Soup and a sandwich.

5. a. Not usually.
   b. On Wednesday night.
   c. No, I don't.

6. a. After five.
   b. Never.
   c. Any time.

6

A Listen and circle the best answer.

1. The conversation is between a . . .
   a. student and his friend.
   b. student and his father.
   c. student and a school counselor.

2. The conversation is about . . .
   a. school sports.
   b. managing time better.
   c. tomorrow's schedule.

3. Paul agrees to . . .
   a. stop volunteering.
   b. stop playing soccer.
   c. stop working at the supermarket.

B Listen again and complete Paul's daily schedule with the activities in the list.

| volunteer work |
| part-time job |
| gets up |
| watches TV |
| classes start |
| homework |
| soccer practice |

8:00 ❶ _____

9:00 ❷ _____

noon
↓ *volunteer work*
1:00

3:00
↓ ❸ _____
4:00

5:00
↓ ❹ _____
8:00

9:00 ❺ _____

11:00
↓ ❻ _____
1:00

7

A Three people are describing their daily routines. Listen and fill in the blanks under *Activity*.

Person	Activity		Time
	gets up		a.
Linda	1.		6:00
	has lunch		b.
	2.		4:00
	gets home		c.
	3.		11:30

Person	Activity	Time
Stewart	leaves home	d.
	4.	9:00
	starts part-time job	e.
	5.	8:00
	watches TV	f.
	6.	11:30
Sophie	**7.**	7:00
	has lunch	g.
	8.	2:00
	meets with council	h.
	9.	6:00
	practices violin	i.

B   **Listen again and fill in the blanks under *Time*.**

C   **Listen again and circle the best answer.**

1. Linda is advised . . .
   a. to choose which team dinner she should attend.
   b. not to go to the team dinners.
   c. to go to the team dinners since it's compulsory.

2. Stewart is advised to . . .
   a. reduce the hours of his part-time job.
   b. quit his part-time job.
   c. change his job to have more free time.

3. Sophie is advised to . . .
   a. give up playing the violin.
   b. give up editing the newspaper.
   c. give up one of her outside activities.

Talking about your daily routine

Sample Dialog

A: What time do you get up in the morning?

B: I get up at about 7:00. Then I take a shower.

A: Do you have breakfast?

B: Yes. I eat and read the paper and then leave home at about 8:15.

A: Maybe you could get up earlier and study English from 7:00 to 7:30.

B: I like to sleep a little later than that, but I guess I could study.

Useful Expressions

- When do you usually **have lunch**?
- Usually at **noon** but sometimes a bit later.
- What do you do **after school**?
- **I watch TV from 7:00 to 8:30** and then **do my homework**.
- Do you have any extra time **in the morning**?
- Could you study **for an hour at lunch**?

Try this . . .

Ask about a partner's daily routine and write the times in the schedule below. Help your partner find some extra time to study English.

Daily Schedule

_____ Get up

_____ Have breakfast

_____ Go to school/work

_____ Have lunch

_____ Get home

_____ Have dinner

_____ Watch TV

_____ Do homework

_____ Go to bed

1 **Complete the sentences using the words in the list. Be sure to use the correct form of the word.**

> make a reservation for   book   be all set for
>
> make it   be just about to   come with

1. Seats must be _____ in advance.
2. I'm sorry. I can't _____ tomorrow.
3. All main courses _____ salad or soup.
4. I _____ the trip.
5. I'd like to _____ two people for Friday night, please.
6. I _____ go out when the phone rang.

2 **Listen. Are these people making reservations or ordering food? Circle _R_ for _reservation_ or _O_ for _ordering food_.**

R / O   R / O   R / O   R / O

3 Listen and circle the correct response.

1. a. I'd like a hot dog, please.
   b. Yes, please.
   c. Yes, I already ordered.

2. a. What kind would you like?
   b. Small or large?
   c. Anything else?

3. a. No, French fries, please.
   b. Medium rare.
   c. No, thanks.

4. a. Root beer, please.
   b. A drink.
   c. Medium, please.

5. a. Sorry, we're full tonight.
   b. How many people?
   c. Around seven o'clock.

6. a. No, the cheeseburger.
   b. Will that be all?
   c. Here's your hamburger.

4

A Listen. How many people are ordering? Circle the number.

CD2
20

1 / 2 / 3 / 4 / 5 / 6

B Listen again and check (✓) the orders.

CD2
20

5

A Listen to the five conversations. Which people are making restaurant reservations? Circle *Yes* or *No*.

	Restaurant reservation?	Successful?
1.	Yes / No	Yes / No / Unknown
2.	Yes / No	Yes / No / Unknown
3.	Yes / No	Yes / No / Unknown
4.	Yes / No	Yes / No / Unknown
5.	Yes / No	Yes / No / Unknown

B Listen again. Which people succeeded in making reservations? Circle *Yes*, *No*, or *Unknown*.

C Listen again and circle the best answer.

1. Harborview café doesn't take reservations . . .
    a. because it is fully booked.
    b. on Saturday night.
    c. on Sunday night.

2. The man wants to make a reservation for . . . at one o'clock.
    a. one person
    b. two people
    c. four people

3. Mr. Chen reserved a meeting room for twelve people at . . . o'clock.
    a. eleven
    b. twelve
    c. one

4. The caller could not make a reservation for three people for . . .
    a. tonight.
    b. tomorrow night.
    c. another night.

5. The woman made a reservation for eight people at . . . o'clock for Saturday night.
    a. seven
    b. eight
    c. nine

Listen and circle the best response.

1. a. Yes, I would.
   b. A hamburger, please.

2. a. No, it doesn't.
   b. Yes, you can.

3. a. Small or large?
   b. Sorry, we're fully booked.

4. a. No, thank you.
   b. Cream and sugar?

5. a. Yes, I did.
   b. Well done, please.

6. a. Two tickets, please.
   b. At 2:30, please.

7

A **Listen and write Jenny's order.**

Surf 'n' Turf
chef's salad

B **Listen again and circle _T_ for _True_ or _F_ for _False_.**

1. Joe had ordered for himself before Jenny arrived. **T / F**
2. For the starter Jenny ordered the fish. **T / F**
3. Both of them ordered the steak. **T / F**
4. They are not sure whether they'll have coffee or not. **T / F**

A Listen and circle *T* for *True*, *F* for *False*, or *U* for *Unknown*.

1. The woman is ordering a meal over the phone.   **T / F / U**
2. The woman is ordering breakfast.   **T / F / U**
3. The woman orders a salad.   **T / F / U**
4. The woman will order dessert.   **T / F / U**

B Listen again and check (✓) the woman's order.

Menu

Burgers

	Plain	$2.95
	Cheese	$3.25
	Double	$3.95
	with cheese	$4.25

Side Orders

	French fries	$1.50
	Onion rings	$1.75
	Baked potato	$1.95

Salads

	Garden	$1.75
	Caesar	$1.95
	Chef's	$1.95

Soups

	Tomato	$1.95
	Onion	$2.25
	Vegetable	$2.25

Drinks

Cola   Diet Cola

	Sm.	$1.25
	Med.	$1.50
	Lg.	$1.95

Desserts

	Apple pie	$1.95
	Cherry pie	$1.95
	with ice cream	$2.50

Ordering food and taking orders

Sample Dialog

A: Are you ready to order?

B: Yes, I'll have the roast beef and a garden salad, please.

A: What kind of dressing would you like?

B: Thousand Island, please.

A: Anything to drink?

B: I'll have an iced tea.

A: OK. Coming right up.

Useful Expressions

• What would you like to order?

• How would you like that done?

• I'd like it **medium rare**, please.

• Did you say **cola**?

• Do you want **milk and sugar** with that?

• Would you like **chocolate** or **red cherry**?

• Would you like anything else?

Try this . . .

Read the menu. Take turns being a restaurant server and a customer.

Menu

Soups
Vegetable ············· $3.50
French Onion ········· $3.95

Salads
Garden Salad ········· $2.95
Caesar Salad ········· $3.95

Main Dishes
Sirloin Steak ········· $9.95
Roast Beef ············ $11.95
Deluxe Burger ········· $6.95
    with cheese ······· $7.50

Desserts
Apple Pie ············· $2.95
    with ice cream ···· $3.50
Cheesecake
    Cherry ············ $3.95
    Chocolate ········· $3.95

Drinks
Cola/Juice/Milk
    small ············· $1.95
    large ············· $2.50
Beer/Wine ············· $3.95 per mug/glass
Coffee/Tea ············ $1.95

1 Complete the sentences using the words in the list. Be sure to use the correct form of the word.

> leader board   lose   defeat   take an early lead   run out   deciding goal

1. France _____ but Wales soon tied the game.
2. We _____ our opponents two to nothing.
3. The Russian team _____ the final game to the U.S.
4. He scored the _____ in the game with England.
5. Ryo Ishikawa remains high on the _____ after the first day of play.
6. My time is _____, like the sand in an hourglass.

2 Match the words in the list to the correct sport. Some words may be used more than once.

_____ _____ _____ _____
_____ _____ _____ _____
_____ _____ _____ _____
_____ _____ _____ _____
_____ _____ _____ _____

> game   serve   field   shoot   green   tackle   pass
>
> court   match   putt   tournament   set   cup   score

3

A Listen and choose the sports you hear from the words in the list.

soccer	golf	tennis	basketball

1. _____ 2. _____ 3. _____ 4. _____

B Listen again and fill in the following blanks.

1. Toronto won by a score of _____ – _____.
2. Kim _____ a stunning upset at the golf championships.
3. The newscaster is going to review the annual _____ tournament and then the hockey matchups.
4. The soccer game was between _____ and Japan.

4

A Listen and circle *T* for *True* or *F* for *False*.

Commentary 1

1. The commentary is at a tennis match.   **T / F**
2. It is a match between two men.   **T / F**
3. The weather is very hot.   **T / F**
4. One of the players is named Jim Stone.   **T / F**

Commentary 2

1. The commentary is at a basketball game.   **T / F**
2. Chang and Wong are on the same team.   **T / F**
3. Wong scores.   **T / F**
4. The game ends.   **T / F**

Commentary 3

1. The commentary is at a golf tournament.   **T / F**
2. Jenny Kim is Australian.   **T / F**
3. The ball is eight feet from the cup.   **T / F**
4. It is raining.   **T / F**

B **Listen again and circle the best answer.**

Commentary 1

1. Which set is about to begin?
   a. The second set
   b. The third set

2. Martinez has some trouble with her . . .
   a. uncle.
   b. ankle.

Commentary 2

1. The ball is passed . . .
   a. from Lee to Chang and then to Wong.
   b. from Lee to Chang and then back to Lee.

2. The score remains . . . at halftime.
   a. 45–50
   b. 45–all

Commentary 3

1. Since the green is still wet after last night's rain, Kim will have to . . .
   a. wait until the green is dry.
   b. hit the shot a little harder.

2. Who is taking the lead?
   a. Jenny Kim
   b. Allie Moran

5   Listen and circle the correct response.

1. a. Yes, I can.
   b. Do you?
   c. Yes, I do.

2. a. I like it, too.
   b. Really? That's great.
   c. Sometimes.

3. a. The gym.
   b. Yes, I do.
   c. Hardly ever.

4. a. I can play on Tuesday.
   b. The golf course.
   c. No, I don't know how.

5. a. How about tomorrow?
   b. I'm not bad.
   c. Do you play?

6. a. Do you? I think it's boring.
   b. So can I.
   c. Every day.

6   A   Listen to the sports broadcasts and fill in the results.

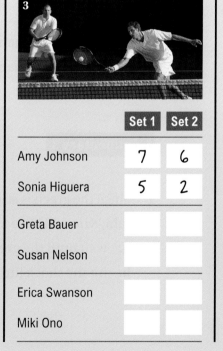

Full-time	
Japan	2
Brazil	1
Italy	
Korea	
Germany	
China	

First Round	
K.S. Kim	64
Peter Miller	
Jiro Ito	
Fred Luciano	
John Lee	
Steve Smith	
Scott Black	

	Set 1	Set 2
Amy Johnson	7	6
Sonia Higuera	5	2
Greta Bauer		
Susan Nelson		
Erica Swanson		
Miki Ono		

B Listen again and circle *T* for *True* or *F* for *False*.

1. At the World Cup, Brazil, Italy, and Germany all lost their games. **T / F**
2. Fred Luciano is low on the leader board after the first day of play. **T / F**
3. Due to heavy rains, many opening round matches were canceled. **T / F**

7

A Listen to the soccer game report and complete the chart.

Team		Score	Team		
	Lords		Woodgate		
Goal Scorers	**Min.**			**Goal Scorers**	**Min.**
1.	21st	3 –	1.	Ian Martin	
2. Dave Smith			2.	David Walker	
3. Alan Nolan					

B Listen again and complete the following scripts.

And now to sports . . . Playing before a crowd of just over ❶_____ fans at Riverside Stadium, the Lords took an early ❷_____ on Mark King's shot from the corner of the penalty area. The goal was . . .

Woodgate ❸_____ the score in the 39th minute, when United midfielder Ian Martin broke a tackle and ❹_____ a shot past West Park keeper Chris Gain. It was . . .

Down but not out, . . . Both teams had chances to win in the next ❺_____ minutes, but with time ❻_____ out, it was West Park striker Alan Nolan who scored the ❼_____ goal. Nolan's . . .

Your Turn!

Talking about sports

Sample Dialog

A: Do you watch a lot of sports on TV?

B: Not really. But I like to play golf.

A: I like golf, too. Are you a good golfer?

B: Yeah, pretty good. How about you?

A: I'm not very good at sports, but I watch a lot of sports on TV.

B: Oh, really? What kinds of sports do you watch?

A: Besides golf, I watch a lot of soccer and tennis matches.

Useful Expressions

- What's your favorite **soccer team**?
- Who's your favorite **basketball player**?
- How often do you go to **baseball games**?
- About **once or twice a month**.
- Do you ever **listen to games on the radio**?
- Do you play on any teams **at school**?

Try this . . .

Ask different classmates the questions below. When someone answers "Yes," write down the person's name. Ask follow-up questions to find out more information.

	Do you . . .	Name	More information
1.	watch a lot of sports on TV?		
2.	read the sports news every day?		
3.	play on a school/company sports team?		
4.	listen to sports on the radio?		
5.	like to go to professional sports events?		

1

Complete the sentences using the words in the list. Be sure to use the correct form of the word.

| contain | postpone | forecast | call | break down | temperature |

1. The excursion has been _____ due to heavy rain.
2. The _____ fell by five degrees.
3. The game was _____ because of rain with the score 1 to 1.
4. It was difficult to _____ the fire because of strong winds.
5. The machines _____ frequently, and it is difficult to get them repaired.
6. According to the weather _____, it will snow tomorrow.

2

Listen and complete the following scripts.

CD2
46
51

1. . . . for Tokyo. And in Seoul it will be _____ with a high of
   _____.

2. And in _____, the Prime Minister said that the Asian Games would be . . .

3. . . . a chance of rain. There will be late _____ in Taipei, with thunder . . .

4. . . . In news just in, authorities in Osaka say that the _____ in a downtown
   shopping mall has been contained.

5. . . . Kuala Lumpur will continue hot and _____ with a high of
   _____ degrees in the . . .

6. . . . spokesman said the president would _____ his upcoming trip to
   Jakarta . . .

3

What is the weather like in Europe? Match each weather report to one of the cities on the map.

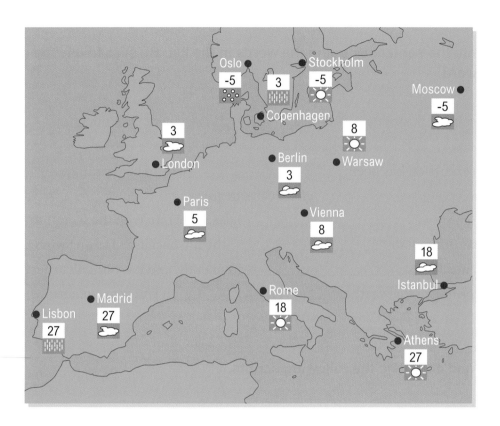

1. . . . rain across the city with the temperature at a very humid twenty-seven degrees . . .

    → _____

2. . . . it's a warm and sunny eighteen degrees in the city this morning . . .

    → _____

3. . . . snow will continue all day, and the temperature will stay at about minus five . . .

    → _____

4. . . . right now, it's partly cloudy with the temperature a cool eight degrees . . .

    → _____

5. . . . cloudy and cold this morning, with a temperature of about minus five degrees . . .

    → _____

4

A Listen and circle the picture that matches each conversation.

1. a.    b.

2. a.    b.

3. a.    b.

B Listen again and answer the following questions.

1. When did they see the Cubs game?

    _____

2. Why couldn't they ski at Ravenwood?

    _____

3. Why was it perfect for sailing?

    _____

5

A Listen to the weather forecasts and write the temperature for each city.

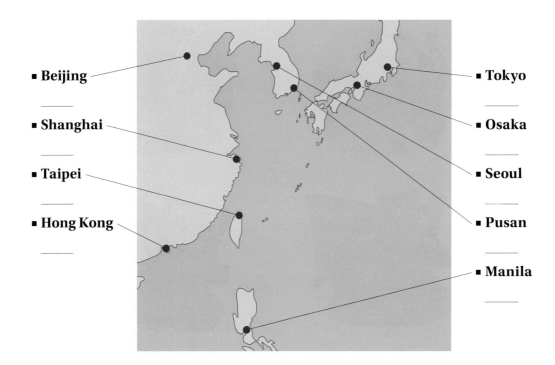

- **Beijing**
  _____
- **Shanghai**
  _____
- **Taipei**
  _____
- **Hong Kong**
  _____

- **Tokyo**
  _____
- **Osaka**
  _____
- **Seoul**
  _____
- **Pusan**
  _____
- **Manila**
  _____

B Listen again and check (✓) the weather in each city.

	sunny	cloudy	rainy
Beijing			
Seoul			
Pusan			
Tokyo			
Osaka			
Shanghai			
Taipei			
Hong Kong			
Manila			

6

Listen and circle the correct response.

CD2
56

1. a. Yes, I know it is.
    b. Yes, it's going to be warm.
    c. Yes, it rains a lot.

2. a. Great. I'm going to the beach today.
    b. No, I heard it's going to rain.
    c. I'd better take an umbrella.

3. a. It's really hot.
    b. Yes, it is.
    c. I really like snowy weather.

4. a. Yeah, I heard that, too.
    b. Good. I like when it rains.
    c. Let's go swimming.

5. a. It's cloudy outside.
    b. Have you seen my umbrella?
    c. Really? I thought it was quite cold.

6. a. Yeah, it's going to be sunny.
    b. I wore my winter coat yesterday.
    c. I don't like it either.

7

A Listen and circle the best answer.

CD2
57

1. This is a weather report for . . .
    a. today.
    b. tomorrow.
    c. the weekend.

2. Rain is forecast in . . .
    a. London, Paris, Madrid.
    b. Rome, Madrid, Paris.
    c. Paris, Rome, Athens.

3. Travelers will need a sweater in . . .
    a. Athens.
    b. Madrid.
    c. London.

B Listen again. Write the temperature and weather below each citiy.

CD2
57

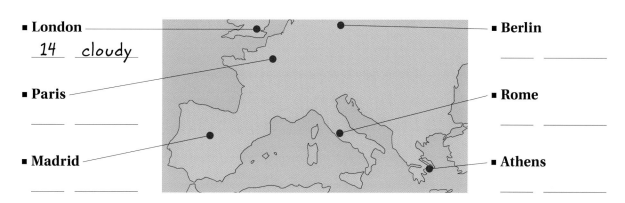

■ **London**
14 cloudy

■ **Paris**
_____ _____

■ **Madrid**
_____ _____

■ **Berlin**
_____ _____

■ **Rome**
_____ _____

■ **Athens**
_____ _____

Your Turn!

Talking about the weather

Sample Dialog

A: Hello, Alison? It's Geoff. I'm calling from Boracay.

B: Geoff! Hi! How's your vacation going?

A: Great! The Philippines is beautiful!

B: How's the weather? I'll bet it's really nice.

A: Yeah, sunny and very hot. I think it's about 33 degrees.

B: Wow, that is hot! What did you do today?

A: We went surfing this morning and scuba diving after lunch.

Useful Expressions

- It's **cold and snowy**.
- What's the temperature?
- I think it's about **10 below**.
- What's the weather forecast for **tomorrow**?
- It's supposed to be **warm and sunny**.
- It's great weather for **skiing**.
- The weather is ideal for **sunbathing**.

Try this . . .

Imagine you are on vacation in one of the cities on the map in Task 5. Write down what the weather is like and two or three things that you did today. Tell a partner. Ask about your partner's vacation.

1 Complete the sentences using the words in the list. Be sure to use the correct form of the word.

go out	blind date	turn out	stay in shape	comfortable	opposite

1. I exercise every day to _____.

2. It _____ that I was right.

3. He is more _____ with computers than with people.

4. He's been _____ with her for two years now.

5. Love is the _____ of hate.

6. She met her husband on a _____.

2 **A** Listen to the three conversations and match each name to the husband's or wife's name.

1. Chuck • • Brad
2. Liz • • Julia
3. Charlotte • • Michael

B Listen again and fill in the following blanks.

1. Chuck met Julia at his _____. After she _____ up with his brother, Chuck and Julia started _____ out.

2. Michael and Liz met at her _____ job. They have been together for _____ years in May.

3. Charlotte met her husband through an _____. After the first date with Bruce, she tried dating another guy who is now her husband.

3 Listen to the conversation and fill in the form.

Name:	Anthony			
Hair:	☐ black	☐ brown	☐ blonde	☐ red
Eyes:	☐ gray	☐ brown	☐ blue	☐ green
Height:	☐ tall	☐ average	☐ short	
Occupation:				
Likes:				

4 **A** Listen to the people describe themselves for a dating agency recording. Check (✓) the information that is true for each person.

	1. Ellen	2. John	3. Shelley	4. Henry	5. Paul	6. Aida
Works at home						
Kind of short						
Wants a tennis partner						
Likes to travel						
Works in a school						
Likes to have fun						
Likes to talk						
Plans to be a doctor						

B Listen again and find each person. Match the names (1–6) to the photos (a–f).

1. Ellen _____
2. John _____
3. Shelley _____
4. Henry _____
5. Paul _____
6. Aida _____

5 Listen and circle the correct response.

1. a. She's kind of tall with brown hair.
   b. Yes, she does.
   c. She likes music.

2. a. Through a dating agency.
   b. About four years ago.
   c. He's an accountant.

3. a. Someone who's outgoing.
   b. Yes, I guess I'm outgoing.
   c. I'm going out now.

4. a. She likes music and going to parties.
   b. Yes, I am. Do you know Jeff Lim?
   c. Yes, it's on the eighteenth.

5. a. Not really.
   b. So do I.
   c. Oh, really? What kind of sports?

6. a. You'd like my sister. She's really funny.
   b. You'd like my sister. She plays badminton, too.
   c. You'd like my sister. She's quite tall.

6

A Listen and circle *T* for *True*, *F* for *False*, or *U* for *Unknown*.

1. She plays tennis twice a week.   **T / F / U**
2. She lives with her parents.   **T / F / U**
3. She likes animals.   **T / F / U**
4. She has short hair.   **T / F / U**

B Listen again and fill in the form.

| Name: | Juliet A. Eastman | | Age: | |

Hair:	☐ black	☐ brown	☐ blonde	☐ red
Eyes:	☐ gray	☐ brown	☐ blue	☐ green
Height:	☐ tall	☐ average	☐ short	

Occupation:

Likes:

Wants to meet someone who:

7

A Listen to the men describe themselves for a dating agency recording. Match the names (1–4) to the photos (a–d).

1. **Andy** _____   2. **Craig** _____   3. **Mel** _____   4. **Stephen** _____

B Listen again and write the activities they like. Use the words in the list.

CD2
70
▼
73

| skiing | swimming | travel | concerts | reading |
| dancing | tennis | parties | movies | volunteering |

1. **Andy**

_____ _____ _____

2. **Craig**

_____ _____ _____

3. **Mel**

_____ _____ _____

4. **Stephen**

_____ _____ _____

8

A Listen as Angela describes the men above. Match the personality traits to the names (1–4).

CD2
74

- **fun-loving** _____   - **quiet** _____
- **talkative** _____   - **impatient** _____
- **shy** _____   - **hardworking** _____
- **athletic** _____   - **serious** _____

B Listen again. What personality traits does she like or dislike? Write the words from the list above.

CD2
74

She likes: _____   **She dislikes:** _____

_____   _____

_____   _____

Your Turn!

Describing yourself

Sample Dialog

A: Could you tell me a little bit about yourself?

B: Well, I'm 31. I'm kind of tall. I have brown hair and green eyes.

A: And how would you describe your personality?

B: I guess I'm kind of an outgoing guy.

A: OK. What kind of person would you like to meet?

B: I'm looking for someone who's also tall, who likes to talk and have fun.

A: I just need to find out a few more things . . .

Useful Expressions

• Could you describe your **appearance** for me?

• I'm about **average height** and I have **blonde** hair.

• I'd like to meet someone who **shares my interests**.

• What sort of things do you do **in your spare time**?

• Does your partner have to **be the same age** as you?

• I want to meet someone **with a good sense of humor**.

Try this . . .

Imagine you work for a dating agency. Your partner phones you and wants to meet someone. Find out about your partner and the kind of person he or she wants to meet. Take notes. Then, switch roles.

■ **Description of client:** _____

_____

_____

_____

■ **Client wants to meet someone who:** _____

_____

_____

_____

Unit 14

Making and changing appointments

1 Complete the sentences using the words in the list. Be sure to use the correct form of the word.

sign up for	appointment	get this straight
reschedule	take a look at	how come

1. I made an _____ to see him in my office tomorrow.
2. The committee meeting has been _____ for three o'clock.
3. _____ you're crying?
4. We will _____ an aerobics class at the club.
5. Let's _____ — you really had no idea where he was?
6. _____ everything that's contributing to your stress.

2

A Listen to the five conversations. What appointments do the people have? Match the conversations (1–5) to the photos (a–e).

1. _____   2. _____   3. _____   4. _____   5. _____

  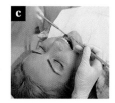  

B Listen again and write the correct day and time for each conversation.

	1.	2.	3.	4.	5.
Day					
Time					

Look at the pictures showing activities in Suzanne's schedule. Use the times and dates under the pictures and the words in the list to fill in Suzanne's planner.

Wed. 5:30–8 p.m.   Tue. 4:30 p.m.   Wed. noon–1 p.m.   Tue. 7:30–9 p.m.

Tue. 10 a.m.   Wed. 3:30 p.m.   Tue. 1:15 p.m.   Wed. 9:30 a.m.

aerobics class	dentist's appointment	debate team meeting
volunteer work	play rehearsal	part-time job
music practice	hair salon appointment	

Tuesday, June 5		Wednesday, June 6	
Time	Activity	Time	Activity
10 a.m.	dentist's appointment		

4

Listen and circle the correct response.

CD2
80

1. **a.** No, not really.
    b. Yes, I'm free all day.
    c. It's tomorrow.

2. **a.** It's on Monday.
    b. Pretty full.
    c. It's from 6:00.

3. **a.** Every weekend.
    b. Tuesday and Thursday.
    c. Friday morning.

4. **a.** Great. Let's go see a movie.
    b. Are you busy then?
    c. That's too bad.

5. **a.** What time is that?
    b. Oh, I forgot.
    c. But I have to go out in the evening.

6. **a.** When does it start?
    b. Are you going?
    c. Oh, really? Why?

5

A ## Listen and circle the best answer.

CD2
81

1. Lydia is calling . . .
    a. a friend.
    b. her teacher.
    c. her boss.

2. She will not be in the office . . .
    a. this afternoon.
    b. tomorrow.
    c. on Monday.

3. Where is the staff meeting going
    to be held?
    a. At the main conference room
    b. At the staff room
    c. At the meeting room

4. What is Mr. Aziz's phone number?
    a. 556–8856
    b. 555–8856
    c. 555–8756

5. Who wants to play golf?
    a. Mrs. Tripplehorn
    b. Mr. Aziz
    c. Mr. Suzuki

6. The staff party is for Mrs. Benchley's . . .
    a. 50th birthday.
    b. 55th birthday.
    c. 15th wedding anniversary.

B Listen again and fill in Mr. Osborne's diary with the activities in the list.

staff meeting   lunch with client   golf game

staff party   dentist's appointment

Fri, May 9

8 A.M. staff meeting

Sat, May 10

6

A Alicia is talking to her mother on the phone. Listen and complete her calendar.

17 FRIDAY	**18** SATURDAY	**19** SUNDAY
4:30 p.m. hair salon appointment	11 a.m.	9:30 a.m.
6 p.m.	1–5:30 p.m.	noon–5 p.m. volunteer work
7:30 p.m. date with Ken	6–10:00 p.m.	7 p.m.

B Listen again and check your answers. When is Alicia planning to visit her family?

CD2
82

7 Hans has to change or cancel some of his appointments this week. Listen to the six conversations and make changes in his planner.

CD2
83
▼
88

7 Mon.	~~Noon — Lunch with Kerry~~
	4–6 p.m. band practice
8 Tue.	11:00 a.m. — Doctor's appointment
	<u>Noon — Lunch with Kerry</u>
	6:30–10 p.m. Play rehearsal
9 Wed.	Art class — 4:00 p.m.
	Band concert @ 8:00 p.m.
10 Thu.	Staff meeting @ 4:30 p.m.
	7:30 p.m. date with Alison
11 Fri.	8 a.m. — Golf with Erin
	1–4 p.m. volunteer at school
12 Sat.	Football team party 9 p.m.
13 Sun.	7:30 p.m. dinner with Mom & Dad

Your Turn!

Making and changing appointments

Sample Dialog

A: Hey, are we still doing that charity fun run on Saturday?

B: Yeah. Oh, but there's a change in the time for the basketball team party on Friday. It's now at 8:00.

A: Really? I'd better write that down.

B: Oh, and I forgot to tell you that basketball practice is canceled this week.

A: So, there's no practice on Tuesday at 4:30?

B: That's right.

Useful Expressions

- What are we doing on **Saturday at 7:30**?
- We're already doing something at that time.
- We have **a study group meeting** on **Wednesday at 3:00**.
- What time are we **playing tennis**?
- **Basketball practice** starts at 4:30.
- How about changing the time to **5:00**?

Try this . . .

Imagine you and your partner are college roommates. The planner shows the activities you're planning to do together this week. Change or cancel some of your plans and tell your partner. Then, switch roles.

Weekly Planner	
Mon.	study group meeting 3:00 P.M.
Tue.	basketball practice 4:30 P.M.
Wed.	tennis game 8:30 A.M.
Thu.	2:00 P.M. volunteer work @ Student Center
Fri.	basketball team party 9:00 P.M.
Sat.	charity fun run @ 7:00 A.M.
Sun.	

1 Complete the sentences using the words in the list.

| pronunciation auditory visual tactile kinesthetic reflective |

1. He is suffering from _____ difficulties because of inflammation of the inner ear.
2. The thick brushstrokes give the painting a _____ quality.
3. _____ learning can be categorized as a style which involves physical activities.
4. _____ people think carefully before making big decisions.
5. I could not understand his _____ of certain words.
6. I did a quick _____ check of the engine.

2 What are the students doing? Use the words in the list to label each picture.

taking notes

listening to a CD

reading a textbook

attending a lecture

asking questions

using a computer

studying in a library

taking part in a discussion

doing an experiment

_____

_____

_____

_____

_____

_____

_____

_____

_____

3 Listen to the lecture on learning styles and complete each sentence. CD2 89

1. Auditory learners learn best by _____.
2. Visual learners learn best by _____.
3. Tactile/Kinesthetic learners learn best by _____.

4 Listen to people describing their study habits. For each person, decide which type of learner they are. Check (✓) *Auditory*, *Visual*, or *Tactile/Kinesthetic*. CD2 90 ▼ 95

1. ☐ Auditory ☐ Visual ☐ Tactile/Kinesthetic
2. ☐ Auditory ☐ Visual ☐ Tactile/Kinesthetic
3. ☐ Auditory ☐ Visual ☐ Tactile/Kinesthetic
4. ☐ Auditory ☐ Visual ☐ Tactile/Kinesthetic
5. ☐ Auditory ☐ Visual ☐ Tactile/Kinesthetic
6. ☐ Auditory ☐ Visual ☐ Tactile/Kinesthetic

5 **A** Anna is answering questions to find out what her learning style is. Listen and number the questions (1–6) in the order you hear them. CD2 96

	Questions	Answers
	How do you learn how a computer works?	
	What's the last book you read for fun?	
	What do you do when you're not sure how to spell a word?	
	How do you study for a test?	
	What do you think of when you hear the word C-A-T?	
	What kind of class did you like best?	

B Listen again and write Anna's answers in the spaces. CD2 96

C **Listen again and circle the best answer.**

CD2
96

1. Anna is being asked about . . .

   a. her listening skill.

   b. her lifestyle.

   c. her learning style.

2. Anna is told to answer . . .

   a. in a couple of seconds.

   b. after careful thought.

   c. what comes to mind most readily.

3. What kind of learner is Anna?

   a. Auditory

   b. Visual

   c. Tactile/Kinesthetic

6

Listen and circle the correct response.

CD2
97

1. **a.** Usually.

   b. Listening.

   c. Yes, I do.

2. **a.** Not very often.

   b. I try to guess.

   c. I prefer speaking.

3. **a.** Yes, I do, but I find it difficult.

   b. No, I prefer reading.

   c. I can't.

4. **a.** I like taking notes.

   b. Yes, they are.

   c. No, it makes me nervous.

5. **a.** Yes, I do.

   b. I'm not sure.

   c. I like learning languages.

6. **a.** Did you guess?

   b. Were you sure?

   c. Was it hard?

7

1. Today is . . .
   a. the first lesson of the semester.
   b. the last lesson of the semester.
   c. the first day of exams.

2. According to the teacher, an active learner . . .
   a. thinks about things very carefully.
   b. likes trying new things out.
   c. enjoys individual problem-solving.

3. The teacher suggests that . . .
   a. active learners are better language learners.
   b. reflective learners are better language learners.
   c. one type of learner is not better than the other.

B   **Listen again and check (✓) your *own* answer (*A* or *B*) to each question you hear.**

1. ☐ **A** contribute a lot of my own ideas
   ☐ **B** listen to my classmates and then give my own opinion

2. ☐ **A** trying it out in conversation with other people
   ☐ **B** thinking carefully about it first, before trying it out

3. ☐ **A** with other people
   ☐ **B** on my own

4. ☐ **A** when everybody brainstorms ideas together
   ☐ **B** when we all think about the issue individually, then compare our ideas

5. ☐ **A** role plays, pair work, and group work
   ☐ **B** individual listening tasks

6. ☐ **A** I get bored quite easily.

   ☐ **B** I find it quite easy to concentrate.

7. ☐ **A** outgoing

   ☐ **B** thoughtful and reserved

C Listen again and check (✓) the kind of learner you are.

CD2
98

☐ I am an active learner.
☐ I am a reflective learner.

8 Three people are talking about the methods they use to improve their listening skills. Listen and fill in the blanks.

CD2
99

Person	Method
Gloria	I listen to a lot of _English songs_. I also spend time ❶_____.
Francisco	One of the things I do is listen to ❷_____. Another is just to walk up to ❸_____ and start a conversation.
Min-hee	I've got all kinds of ❹_____ that I use to practice. Oh, I also listen to the ❺_____ on the radio.

Your Turn!

Asking and talking about learning styles

Sample Dialog

A: Do you tend to learn a lot in lectures?

B: Not really. I usually can't remember much from lectures.

A: What if the lecturer draws diagrams on the board?

B: Yeah, that makes it easier. I also learn more when I draw my own diagrams.

A: Do you like to study from textbooks?

B: Sometimes. It helps if the textbook has a lot of illustrations.

A: Sounds like you're a visual learner.

Useful Expressions

• Do you prefer to **read a textbook** or **listen to a lecture**?

• I learn a lot more when I **listen to a lecture**.

• Are you better at **using a map** or **listening to directions**?

• I'm better at **using a map**. I can't **remember directions**.

• What's the easiest way for you to learn something?

• Do you think **role-plays** help you to learn?

Try this . . .

Interview your partner about his/her learning experiences and preferences. Use the words below to help you. Write down your partner's responses.

- **Lectures**
- **Demonstrations**
- **Map-reading**
- **Textbooks**
- **Studying for tests**
- **Class projects**
- **Graphs and diagrams**

クラス用音声 CD 有り（非売品）

Hear Me Out 1 [Text Only]

実践リスニング徹底演習シリーズ＜初級編＞

2017年1月20日　初版発行
2024年4月10日　Text Only版第2刷

著　者　David Nunan
編著者　富岡紀子
発行者　松村達生
発行所　センゲージ ラーニング株式会社
　　　　〒102-0073　東京都千代田区九段北1-11-11　第2フナトビル5階
　　　　電話 03-3511-4392　FAX 03-3511-4391
　　　　e-mail: eltjapan@cengage.com
　　　　copyright©2017 センゲージ ラーニング株式会社

装　丁　　　足立友幸（parastyle）
編集協力　　飯尾緑子（parastyle）
印刷・製本　株式会社平河工業社

ISBN 978-4-86312-317-5